# of Recipes

As a result of your many requests here
is my fourth book of recipes, all of which
have been shown on the BBC Television
Programmes 'Town and Around' and 'Look East'.
It contains a hundred new recipes
which have been demonstrated during the
twelve-month period up to May of this year,
when the book went to the printers.
You will notice that I have included
more meat, pastry and savoury recipes, as
I find these are very popular with you.
I also receive a lot of correspondence
from children who enjoy making the more
simple recipes, and most of these can be
found under the biscuit section.
Once again I have tried to include
recipes to suit a variety of tastes, using
as far as possible everyday ingredients, and
I do hope you will enjoy trying them.
My grateful thanks go to everyone
connected with the programmes and the
production of this book. To my mother and
father who help in so many ways and to
'you' the viewers, for your continued
interest in these programmes.

*Zena Skinner*

# Zena Skinner's Fourth Book of Recipes

Illustrated by Juliet Renny

British Broadcasting Corporation

Published by the
British Broadcasting Corporation
35 Marylebone High Street
London W.1

SBN: 563 07350 0

First published 1967

Printed and bound in Great Britain by
Hazell Watson & Viney Ltd
Aylesbury, Bucks

# Contents

7

# Herbs and Spices

There are many varieties of herb and spice racks available, some use glass jars for storage and others come in metal containers.

It is important for all herbs and spices to be kept in containers with well-fitting lids, this preserves their flavours. It is also important to keep strong light away from herbs and spices stored in glass jars, as this preserves the colour.

Here are some ways of using a few of the better known herbs and spices, which can add extra flavour to your cooking.

### HERBS

*Bay Leaves*

These come from the true laurel tree and when dried have a strong flavour, so they should be used cautiously.

By adding just the right amount they can improve the flavouring of the following: soups, stews, sauces, salad dressings (i.e. oil and vinegar ones), fish, meat (i.e. roasting, marinading and when cooking bacon joints), poultry, game, rice and pasta dishes.

## Bouquet Garni

This name is given to a small bunch of herbs, which in its simplest form contains a sprig of thyme, marjoram, a bay leaf and parsley, all of which are tied in a small muslin bag.

However, today it is easy to purchase bouquet garni in a tea-bag type sachet. In this case the spices have already been blended by the manufacturer and the sachets usually contain parsley, chervil, marjoram, thyme and bay leaf. One sachet put into a soup, casserole or marinade will certainly enrich the flavour.

## Marjoram

The variety used for cooking is known as sweet knotted marjoram, and it has a strong, sweet, spicy flavour.

It should be used sparingly, particularly if you have not used it before.

Particularly good for stuffings and in meat dishes, either rubbed into the meat before it is roasted or in made-up meat dishes. It can also be rubbed on the inside of poultry and game before roasting and a small amount will also improve the flavour of egg, cheese, soup, stews and fish dishes.

## Sage

Use only first-class quality sage, as only then does it have a pungent flavour and should be used with discretion.

We all know the use of this herb with onion as a stuffing for pork and duck, but there are many more ways in which it can be used.

Here are a few examples: fish, liver, game, cream or cottage cheese, sausage dishes and soups.

If you are making a summer fruit drink a very little sage gives it a delicious flavour.

## Tarragon

This herb should be used sparingly and is an essential ingredient in rich sauces and chicken dishes.

The following dishes can also be improved in flavour with the careful use of tarragon: shellfish cocktails, salads, lamb, mutton or pork, as a herb butter on steaks and also with soup and egg dishes.

## Thyme

A very strong herb and therefore must only be used in small quantities. It is an essential ingredient of a 'bouquet garni' and is used a great deal in fat meat dishes such as mutton and pork.

Other foods which can be improved in flavour by a small addition of this herb are shellfish, egg and cheese dishes, and in the stuffing of most poultry and game.

With regard to vegetables, blend a very little with some butter and toss the vegetables in it before serving. Suggested vegetables are carrots, asparagus, mushrooms, onions and potatoes.

### SPICES

## Cayenne Pepper

This is prepared from the capsicum pepper and is therefore very hot, so use it carefully.

It is particularly good used in cheese dishes to bring out the flavour, and also in other savoury dishes.

Its colour is bright red and can be confused with paprika pepper which is almost the same colour.

## Cinnamon

This can be purchased ground or in stick form and in the latter is useful for flavouring liquids used in puddings and sauces.

The ground variety is used mainly for flavouring cakes, stews and savoury dishes; also puddings, sauces and chutneys.

## Cloves

Some years ago I was in Zanzibar when the clove harvest was in progress and the smell was almost overpowering from the dried flowerbuds. They have a pungent flavour and can be bought whole or powdered.

The use of whole cloves when cooking bacon and ham are well known, as is the onion stuck with cloves that goes into the stewpot. When it comes to puddings and cakes I favour the powdered form, but use it very sparingly, so that it enhances the flavour and doesn't kill it.

11

## Ginger

There are three varieties – ground, crystallized and whole pickling (root).

Ground ginger is used by people who find that sliced or chopped ginger is offensive in flavouring cakes and puddings. It is also used in some savoury dishes and is often served as an accompaniment to curry.

Crystallized, is used in the main, sliced or chopped in cakes, puddings and stewed fruit dishes, i.e. Rhubarb and Ginger.

Whole pickling (root), as its name implies, is used in the making of pickles. I also use it for making marrow and ginger preserves.

Before using it crush or bruise it to allow the flavour to come out and tie it in a small piece of muslin before adding it to the other ingredients.

## Mace and Nutmeg

I class these two together as mace is the outer shell or husk of the nutmeg and therefore they resemble each other in flavour.

Mace can be bought in blade form or ground and it is orange-yellow in colour. Nutmeg is bought whole or ground.

They are both used to flavour sweet and savoury sauces, cakes, puddings, stuffings, stews and potatoes. It is also traditional in Britain to grate it on top of milk puddings, junkets and custards.

Both of these spices should be used with discretion.

# Cakes and Loaves

## 1. WEDDING CAKE

This recipe comes as a result of your many requests for a wedding cake, using the same ingredients as I did for the Christmas Cake in 1964.

**INGREDIENTS**

12 oz. raisins
1 lb. 2 oz. currants
1 lb. 2 oz. sultanas
4½ oz. chopped blanched almonds
4½ oz. chopped angelica
6 oz. quartered glacé cherries
6 oz. chopped candied peel
15 oz. plain flour
15 oz. butter

15 oz. Barbados type brown sugar
7 standard eggs
Grated **rind** 1½ lemons
4 tablespoonsful brandy or rum
1½ level teaspoonsful mixed spice
Pinch nutmeg
Pinch salt

METHOD: Line the cake tin with a double thickness of greased greaseproof paper. Tie a double thickness band of brown paper round the outside of the tin and secure with string. Clean the fruit if necessary, and sieve together the flour, spices and salt.

Cream the butter and sugar together until light and fluffy, beat in the eggs one at a time, adding a tablespoonful of sieved flour with each egg. Add all other ingredients a little at a time except for the brandy or rum, stirring until all the ingredients are evenly blended. Finally add the spirit and a little milk if the mixture is too stiff, it should just drop off the spoon easily. Bake at approximately 300° F or mark 1–2 for 4 to 4½ hours. To test when cooked, place a thin steel knitting needle into the cake several times in different places and if the needle comes out clean the cake is cooked. Turn out on to a wire cooling tray and when really cold, preferably the next day, wrap in grease-proof paper or foil and seal in a tin. This will allow the cake to mature well before being iced. (12″ round cake)

## WEDDING CAKES

INGREDIENTS

### Both Cakes

8 oz. raisins
12 oz. currants
12 oz. sultanas
3 oz. chopped blanched
  almonds
3 oz. chopped angelica
4 oz. quartered glacé cherries
4 oz. chopped candied peel
10 oz. plain flour
10 oz. butter

10 oz. Barbados type brown
  sugar
5 standard eggs
Grated rind 1 lemon
3 tablespoonsful brandy
  or rum
1 level teaspoonful
  mixed spice
Small pinch nutmeg
Pinch salt

METHOD: Make in exactly the same way as for the larger cake. Then put two-thirds of the mixture into the 8½″ tin and the remaining mixture into the 6″ tin.

### Baking times

For 8½″ cake approximately 300° F or mark 1–2 for about 3½ hours.

For 6″ cake approximately 300° F or mark 1–2 for about 2½ hours.

Store as stated for larger cake.

(8½″ cake and 6″ cake)

14

## 2. BATTENBURG CAKE

If you don't like fruit cake, but do like marzipan, this may be the cake for you.

**INGREDIENTS**

*Cake*

6 oz. butter
6 oz. castor sugar
3 large eggs
Few drops vanilla essence

6 oz. self-raising flour
1 level tablespoonful cocoa
Small quantity jam

*Coating*

1 lb. almond paste

METHOD: Grease a tin approximately 11″ × 7″. Line the tin with greased greaseproof paper, making a double fold down the centre of the tin. Cream the butter and sugar together until light and fluffy, then gradually beat in the eggs and essence. Fold in the flour and when evenly blended put half the mixture into one side of the tin. Add the cocoa to the remaining mixture and when blended put into the other side of the tin. Bake at approximately 375° F or mark 4 for about 35 minutes.

When cooked, cool on wire trays, and when cold trim each half into 2 equal sized squares and sandwich together with jam into a chequerboard design. Roll the almond paste out to cover all four sides of the cake, spread with a little jam and press the paste on to the cake. Crimp the top edges and mark a pattern on the top using the back of a knife.     (12 portions)

## 3. CHOCOLATE ORANGE SPONGE CAKE

An easy-to-make sponge cake and the filling and icing can be varied to suit personal taste and special occasions.

**INGREDIENTS**

3 standard eggs
3 oz. castor sugar

3 oz. self-raising flour
1 level tablespoonful cocoa

*Filling*

5 oz. butter
10 oz. sieved icing sugar
Finely grated rind 1 medium-
  sized orange

Approximately dessertspoonful fresh orange juice

METHOD: Grease and dust with flour two 7″ sponge sandwich tins. Whisk together in a basin the sugar and eggs until thick and creamy, so that when the beater is lifted a distinct trail is left across the surface of the mixture. Fold in gently the sieved flour and cocoa. When evenly blended divide the mixture evenly between the tins and bake at approximately 425° F or mark 8 for 12–15 minutes. Cool on wire trays and allow to become quite cold before filling.

*To make the filling:* Cream the butter and icing sugar together until soft and fluffy, add the grated rind of the orange and sufficient of the orange juice to flavour. Spread half the mixture on the sponge for the filling and spread a layer on top of the sponge. Use the remaining mixture to pipe a decoration on the cake.

N.B. If a coffee filling is preferred use the same amount of butter and icing sugar and add approximately 1 level teaspoonful of instant coffee. (7″ cake)


## 4. LEMON AND ALMOND CAKE

A recipe suitable for coffee or tea time and one that should sell at the local Bazaar.

INGREDIENTS

3 oz. butter or margarine
3 oz. dark soft brown sugar
Grated rind of 1 lemon

1 standard egg yolk
4 oz. plain flour
12 whole blanched almonds

METHOD: In a basin cream together the butter or margarine and sugar until light and fluffy. Add the grated lemon rind and egg yolk and beat well. Work in the sieved flour until evenly blended and spread the mixture into a 7″ greased sponge sandwich tin. Arrange the almonds in a pattern on the top. Bake at approximately 325° F or mark 2 for about 40 minutes. When cooked allow to stand in the tin for a few minutes then mark into 8 pieces and cool on a wire tray.

(8 portions)


## 5. DEVIL'S FOOD CAKE

A delicious chocolate cake with a honey and orange flavour.


INGREDIENTS

4 level tablespoonsful clear honey
2 oz. plain chocolate
8 oz. butter

4 oz. castor sugar
4 standard eggs
8 oz. self-raising flour


*Filling*

3 oz. butter
3 oz. icing sugar

Few drops fresh orange juice


*Icing*

1½ oz. butter

3 oz. icing sugar


METHOD: Place the honey and chocolate in a small basin over a pan of hot water. Stir until the chocolate has melted, then allow to cool. Cream butter and sugar until light and fluffy, beat in the honey mixture, and then the eggs one at a time. Fold in the sieved flour carefully. Divide the mixture equally between two 9″ sandwich tins which have been greased round the side and have a circle of greased paper in the base. Bake at approximately 375° F or mark 4–5 for about 30–35 minutes. Cool on wire racks.

*To make the filling:* Cream the butter and icing sugar well together until light and fluffy, add the juice and spread on the sponge cakes.

*To make the icing:* Cream the butter and sugar as for the filling, spread evenly over the top of the cake, and make a design with the back of a fork.

(8 portions)

# 6. TEA-TIME FINGERS

A good cake to make for coffee parties, or for the cake stall of your local Women's group.

INGREDIENTS

4 oz. butter
5 oz. Demerara sugar
2 large eggs
6 oz. self-raising flour
½ teaspoonful vanilla essence

4 oz. chocolate dots
2 oz. sultanas
4 oz. walnuts (coarsely chopped)

METHOD: Grease a tin approximately 11″ × 7″. In a basin cream together the butter and sugar, add the eggs and beat again. Stir in the remaining ingredients and mix well.

When evenly blended turn the mixture into the prepared tin. Bake at approximately 350° F or mark 3 for about 40 minutes. Cool in the tin. When cold cut into fingers.          (20 portions)


# 7. MILLIE'S FRUIT LOAF

For this recipe washing up is kept to a minimum. The loaf keeps fresh, if allowed to, for a week.

INGREDIENTS

*The cup I used held 8 fluid oz. of water*

1 teacupful cold tea
1 teacupful granulated sugar
1 teacupful mixed dried fruit

2 oz. butter or margarine
1 large egg
2 teacupsful self-raising flour

METHOD: In a saucepan put the tea, sugar, butter and fruit, bring to simmering point and simmer for 2–3 minutes. Take the pan from the heat and allow to cool until lukewarm, then add the beaten egg and sieved flour. Mix all well together with a wooden spoon, and pour into a greased and lined 2-lb. loaf tin. Bake at approximately 350° F or mark 4 for 1–1¼ hours. Turn out and allow to get cold on a cooling rack before storing in an airtight tin.

## 8. LINCOLNSHIRE FRUIT LOAF

This recipe was given to me by a friend of the family, it's quick to make and keeps well if allowed to!

INGREDIENTS

| | |
|---|---|
| 12 oz. mixed dried fruit including peel | 7½ fluid oz. cold tea |
| | 1 large egg |
| 4 oz. Demerara sugar | 8 oz. self-raising flour |

METHOD: In a basin mix together the fruit, sugar and cold tea, cover with a cloth and leave to stand overnight.

*The following day*

Well grease and line with greaseproof paper a 2-lb. loaf tin.

Lightly beat the egg and stir into the fruit mixture, finally adding the sieved flour. Stir until the mixture is evenly blended, then put it into the prepared tin and bake at approximately 350° F or mark 3–4 for 1¼–1½ hours.

The loaf is baked when the top is firm to the touch, and it has started to shrink from the sides of the tin.    (2-lb. loaf)


## 9. PINEAPPLE AND NUT BREAD

This bread was made as my contribution in support of the Empire and Commonwealth Games in Jamaica.

INGREDIENTS

| | |
|---|---|
| 8-oz. can pineapple pieces (chopped) | 3 level tablespoonsful black treacle |
| 2 oz. walnuts (chopped) | 1 standard egg |
| 4 oz. butter | 12 oz. self-raising flour |
| 2 oz. castor sugar | |

*Icing*

| | |
|---|---|
| 3 oz. sieved icing sugar | Few whole walnuts |
| 1 tablespoonful pineapple juice | |

METHOD: Slightly warm the treacle before measuring, to ensure an accurate measurement. Drain the can of pineapple and keep the juice. In a basin cream together the butter, sugar and treacle until light in colour and fluffy. Gradually beat in the lightly beaten egg. Fold in the sieved flour, pineapple, walnuts and 4 tablespoonsful of the pineapple juice.

When evenly blended divide the mixture in half and put into 2 greased and lined 1-lb. loaf tins, levelling off the top. Bake at approximately 325° F or mark 2 for 1–1¼ hours. When firm to the touch and evenly browned turn out and cool on a wire tray.

*To make the icing:* Sieve the icing sugar into a small basin, and mix with the pineapple juice. When evenly blended, spread over the top of the bread and decorate with the whole walnuts.

(2 × 1-lb. loaves)

## 10. NELLIE'S TEA CAKES

Here are yeast buns with a fruity flavour, and I like to eat them hot.

### INGREDIENTS

| | |
|---|---|
| 1 lb. self-raising flour | 1 oz. compressed yeast, |
| 1 oz. lard | *or* ½ oz. dried yeast |
| 4 oz. mixed dried fruit | Pinch salt |
| ½ oz. chopped candied peel | Approximately ⅓ pint warm |
| 1½ oz. castor sugar | milk to mix |

METHOD: Sieve the flour into a basin and rub in the lard. Add fruit, peel and salt. Mix the yeast and sugar together until the yeast becomes liquid. Add one-third of a pint of warm milk to the yeast mixture, stir together and pour into the dry ingredients. Mix all well together with a spoon or the hand until the mixture leaves the sides of the basin. Cover with a piece of polythene or a cloth and set in a warm place to rise about 1½ hours or until the mixture has doubled its size.

Turn the mixture out on to a floured board and knead well with the heel of the hand until the mixture is pliable and not sticky. Divide equally into 12 pieces, mould into round buns, place on warmed baking tins, cover and allow to rise to double their size about ½ hour. Bake at approximately 400° F or mark 6 for 10–15 minutes. When baked the buns should be golden brown on top, and sound hollow when tapped with the fingers on the base. Serve spread with butter, or if a day or two old toasted with butter. (12 cakes)

## 11. ORANGE LOAF

This can be eaten as a cake when freshly baked or spread with butter as a loaf when a few days old.

INGREDIENTS

| | |
|---|---|
| 2 oz. butter | 3 tablespoonsful orange juice |
| 6 oz. castor sugar | 2 tablespoonsful milk |
| 1 large egg (beaten) | 7 oz. self-raising flour |
| ½ large orange (grated rind) | Large pinch salt |

METHOD: Grease and line a 2-lb. loaf tin with greased grease-proof paper. Cream the butter until very soft and then work in the sugar until evenly blended. Add the egg and beat, also the milk and orange rind.

Sieve the flour and salt into the mixture and stir in, adding the orange juice as you go. Put the mixture into the prepared tin and spread evenly on the top. Bake at approximately 375° F or mark 4–5 for 50 minutes to 1 hour, when the loaf should have started to shrink from the sides of the tin. Turn out and cool on a wire tray. (2-lb. loaf)

# Biscuits

## 12. PINWHEEL BISCUITS

If you have a refrigerator, you can make these up well in advance, and cook them when unexpected guests arrive. They can even watch you do them!

**INGREDIENTS**

*Plain mix*

2 oz. plain flour
2 oz. butter
1 oz. cornflour

1 oz. castor sugar
1 tablespoonful milk

*Coffee mix*

2 oz. plain flour
2 oz. butter
1 oz. cornflour

1 oz. castor sugar
1 tablespoonful coffee
  essence

22

METHOD: Using two basins soften the butter, using 2 oz. in each basin. Add the remaining ingredients of the plain mix into one basin and the coffee ingredients into the other. Work the mixtures together until each is evenly blended. Lightly flour a board and roll each mix out separately into an oblong shape. When they are even in size, brush the plain mix lightly with a little milk, and place the coffee oblong on the top. Press lightly together with a rolling pin, then roll up as for a swiss roll. Wrap the roll in foil or waxed paper and place in the refrigerator on a smooth surface, i.e. the base.

When the biscuits are required, which can be anything up to a week, cut into slices about $\frac{1}{8}''$ in thickness and place on greased baking tins. Bake at approximately 350° F or mark 3–4 for 12–15 minutes, until lightly golden brown. Allow them to cool on the tins for a little while, then store in an airtight tin on their own. (Approx. 2 dozen)

## 13. NUTTY SQUARES

Here's a favourite with the children as it's nice and sweet, but don't let them have too much!

INGREDIENTS

6-oz. packet Maryland cookies
2 oz. butter

4 level tablespoonsful golden syrup
4 level tablespoonsful crunchy peanut butter

METHOD: Grease a 7" square tin. Crush cookies with a rolling pin. Melt the butter in a saucepan over a gentle heat, add syrup and bring to the boil. Stir in the peanut butter until evenly blended. Remove the pan from the heat, add the cookies and mix well. Press these ingredients into the greased tin and leave in a cool place until firm. Cut into squares when cold.

(16 squares)

## 14. CHOCOLATE COFFEE CRISPS

Here's a recipe the older children can make on a wet day, during the holidays.

23

INGREDIENTS

1 packet chocolate dots

1 level teaspoonful instant
coffee powder

1 oz. puffed rice cereal
(Rice Crispies)

METHOD: Melt the chocolate and coffee powder in a basin over a pan of hot water. When smooth, remove the pan from the heat and stir in the cereal. When the cereal is evenly coated, pile into waxed cake cases and allow to set.     (Approx. 10)


## 15. NO-BAKE PEANUT SQUARES

Children love these and the older ones can easily make them.

INGREDIENTS

2 oz. butter
1 oz. castor sugar
3 level tablespoonsful
golden syrup

3 oz. crunchy peanut butter
6 oz. semi-sweet biscuits

METHOD: Roughly crush the biscuits with a rolling pin. In a saucepan melt the butter over a gentle heat. Add the sugar and syrup and bring to the boil. Remove the pan from the heat immediately and stir in the peanut butter. When evenly blended add the biscuits and work into the syrup. Press the mixture into a greased 7″ square tin and leave to cool. When almost cold cut into 16 squares and allow to get quite cold.

(16 squares)


## 16. CHOCOLATE RAISIN CRUNCHIES

Here's a recipe the older children can make, perhaps for their own parties or to help mother.

INGREDIENTS

6 oz. plain or milk chocolate
6 oz. seedless raisins

1 oz. cornflakes
1 oz. toasted sliced almonds

METHOD: Melt the chocolate in a basin over hot water. Remove from the heat and add the remaining ingredients, stirring until they are all coated. Put teaspoonsful of the mixture on to waxed paper and allow to set.     (16–18 portions)

# 17. PEEL AND ALMOND COOKIES

Here's a tip – chop the almonds and peel together as it is so much quicker as the almonds stick to the peel but the peel doesn't stick to the knife!

INGREDIENTS

2 oz. butter
2 oz. finely chopped
   blanched almonds

2 oz. finely chopped mixed
   peel
2 oz. castor sugar
1½ oz. plain flour

METHOD: In a basin beat the butter until soft and creamy, add almonds, peel and sugar and mix well together. Add flour and work into the other ingredients until it all binds together and leaves the sides of the basin clean.

Break off pieces about the size of a walnut, roll in the hands and place on greased baking sheets, leaving room for the cookies to spread. Finally flatten each one with the back of a fork. Bake at approximately 350° F or mark 3–4 for 12–15 minutes when the edges will be turning golden brown. Leave on the tins to cool for a few minutes then transfer them on to wire cooling trays. Store in an airtight tin *away* from other biscuits or cakes.                    (16 cookies)

# 18. HONEY CLUSTERS

The older children will enjoy making these and they do not need the oven for cooking.

INGREDIENTS

2 oz. butter
2 oz. castor sugar

3 level tablespoonsful
   clear honey
3 oz. Rice Crispies

METHOD: In a saucepan melt the butter and sugar, and boil for 30 seconds. Remove the pan from the heat and stir in the honey. Finally add the Crispies and stir well until they are evenly coated.

Spoon the mixture into paper cases and allow to get quite cold. Store in an airtight tin on their own.    (18–20 clusters)

# Pastries and Savouries

## 19. CANDIED XMAS TREE

Here we have an Xmas tree made with pastry and it looks very attractive on the table.

**INGREDIENTS**

*Base*

6 oz. rough puff pastry.

*Filling and topping*

1½ oz. currants
¾ oz. candied peel
¾ oz. chopped angelica
¾ oz. chopped glacé cherries
1¼ oz. Demerara sugar

METHOD: In a basin mix well together all the ingredients for the filling. Divide the pastry in half and roll out two equal triangles approximately 8″ long by 5″ wide at the base. Place one triangle on a greased baking tin and cut a strip from the base ¾″ wide, fold this in half and place slightly overlapping at the base to form the trunk of the tree.

Damp all round the edge with a little water. Sprinkle half of the filling evenly over the triangle on the baking tin, leaving a ¼″ space round the edge.

Place the second triangle on top of the first, and seal the edges well together.

Brush the top of the pastry with a little beaten egg or milk. With a sharp knife cut six slits on either side, leaving a central main stem. Ease the branches slightly apart from each other, then lightly press out the centre of each branch and top with the remainder of the filling.

Bake at approximately 475° F or mark 8–9 for about 12–15 minutes, when the top should be golden brown. When cold you could decorate with a little glacé icing to resemble snow.

## 20. SAUSAGE SUPPER DISH

A quickly made supper dish for the busy housewife, and also suitable for wives out at work all day.

INGREDIENTS

1 lb. beef sausages
1 (1 pint) packet thick onion soup
¾ pint cold water

¾ lb. peeled potatoes (cut into ½″ dice)
1 small packet frozen peas
Seasoning to taste

METHOD: Gently fry the sausages until golden brown all over, about 15 minutes. In the meantime make up the soup as directed on the packet, but using *¾ pint of water only*. When it comes to the boil add the potatoes and simmer for 10 minutes. Add the cooked peas and drained sausages, and simmer with the lid on until the potatoes are cooked, about 10 minutes. Serve at once.


## 21. BANBURY CAKES

There are many recipes for these cakes but this one is my personal favourite. Once baked, they can be heated up several days later if required.

INGREDIENTS

8 oz. rough puff pastry

*Filling*

2 oz. butter
2 oz. castor sugar
4 oz. currants
Grated rind ½ lemon
1 oz. chopped candied peel
Small pinch cinnamon

Small pinch mixed spice
Yolk of 1 standard egg
1 dessertspoonful brandy
*or*
1 tablespoonful sherry

METHOD: *Filling:* Beat the butter and sugar together until light and fluffy. Add all the other ingredients for the filling except for the brandy or sherry. When blended together add the spirit and mix well again. Allow this mixture to stand while rolling out or making the pastry.

27

Roll out the pastry to about $\frac{1}{8}$" thickness and cut into 5" or 6" rounds, about the size of a small saucer. Place a heaped teaspoonful of the filling in the centre of each round. Moisten the edges with a little beaten egg white, fold over two sides of the pastry until they overlap in the centre. Press lightly together and seal the two ends, form into boat shapes. Flatten cakes slightly, turn them over and brush with a little beaten egg white and dredge with castor sugar. Make two or three slits on the top. Bake at approximately 425° F or mark 8 for about 15 minutes, when the tops will be crisp and brown. Serve either hot or cold. (Approx. 9 cakes)

## 22. SAVOURY EGG PASTIES

Delicious eaten hot or cold, so can be taken on a picnic. If you haven't tried fried short crust pastry before, I hope you will like it.

INGREDIENTS

8 oz. short crust pastry
3 large hard-boiled eggs
1 small egg (beaten)
Little Marmite

Little horseradish
Little chutney
Oil or fat for frying

METHOD: Roll the pastry out and cut into six 6" circles (about the size of a saucer). Spread the pastry with the Marmite, horseradish or chutney fairly generously, leaving 1" clear all round the edge. Cut each egg in half lengthwise, and place one piece on each circle, slightly to one side. Brush the edges with the beaten egg, fold over the other half of the pastry, and well seal the edges. Decorate the edges in different ways so that you can tell the different fillings.

Heat $\frac{1}{2}$" of fat or oil in a deep frying pan, put in the pasties and fry until the pastry is golden brown allowing $3\frac{1}{2}$–4 minutes on each side. The pastry must not be cooked too quickly otherwise it will not be cooked inside. Serve hot or cold.

(6 portions)

## 23. EGG AND ONION CASSEROLE

I had a cold coming on at the time I made this dish, but the onions cured it.

INGREDIENTS

1½ oz. butter
½ lb. onions (thinly sliced)
¾ oz. cornflour
1 pint milk
Salt and pepper to taste

Pinch grated nutmeg
2 tablespoonsful white wine
4 large hard-boiled eggs
4 portions mashed potatoes

METHOD: Melt the butter in a saucepan, add the onions and fry gently until tender and transparent, but do not allow them to brown. While the onions are frying, pipe the mashed potatoes in a border round a deep ovenproof dish, brush with a little beaten egg or milk, and brown under the grill. Keep this dish hot.

Blend the cornflour with a little milk, add to the onions stirring all the time. Gradually add the remaining milk, and continue cooking for a further 12–15 minutes stirring frequently.

Add the seasonings, nutmeg and wine and when blended stir in 3 coarsely chopped eggs.

Pour these ingredients into the prepared dish, garnish with the remaining hard-boiled egg and a little chopped parsley. Serve at once.                                              (4 portions)

## 24. HAM AND TURKEY CROQUETTES

These were made to use up the turkey and ham after Xmas, but made with bacon they are a good breakfast dish at any time.

INGREDIENTS

½ lb. minced, cooked turkey
and ham
2 teaspoonsful fresh lemon
juice
Salt and pepper to taste

1 standard egg (beaten)
Little plain flour
Browned breadcrumbs
Fat or oil for frying

29

*Sauce*

1 oz. plain flour                        $\frac{1}{4}$ pint milk
1 oz. butter

METHOD: Make a thick white sauce by melting the 1 oz. of butter and stirring in the 1 oz. of plain flour. Allow time for these to cook approximately 2 minutes without the flour browning, remove the pan from the heat and gradually add the milk. Bring to the boil then add turkey, ham, lemon juice and seasoning to taste. When all well blended, spread the mixture on to a plate and allow to get quite cold.

Divide the mixture into 6 equal portions and mould into round or oval shapes with a little flour. Brush well with beaten egg and coat in the breadcrumbs. Deep fat fry for about 1 minute on each side until golden brown in colour. Drain on absorbent paper and keep hot until ready to serve.

N.B. If using these for breakfast make them up the night before and fry at breakfast time. If turkey and ham are not available cooked minced bacon may be used in their place.

(6 portions)


## 25. BACON AND POTATO PUFF

A tasty lunch or supper dish, using up the odd pieces left from a bacon joint.

*Ingredients*

1 packet instant mashed          2 tablespoonsful milk
  potato                         Pinch basil
Salt and pepper                  6 oz. cooked minced bacon
1 large egg (separated)          2 tomatoes (skinned and
$\frac{1}{2}$ small teaspoonful ready-          chopped)
  made mustard                   Little melted butter

METHOD: Lightly grease a 1-pint soufflé dish. Season the mashed potatoes then fold in the stiffly beaten egg white.

Beat together the egg yolk, mustard, milk and basil, add to the bacon and tomatoes, season with pepper and stir until evenly blended. Put this mixture into the base of the prepared dish, cover with the potato, smoothing the top then brush with melted butter.

Bake at approximately 425° F or mark 8 for 35–45 minutes until golden brown. Serve hot with vegetables or a salad.

(4 portions)

## 26. CRISPY BACON BITES

An inexpensive dish quickly made and more than likely you'll have all the ingredients already in the larder.

INGREDIENTS

3 rashers of English streaky bacon
1 raw peeled potato about 4 oz. in weight (grated)
1 small onion (chopped)

1 standard egg
1 oz. self-raising flour
Pepper to taste
Fat for frying

METHOD: Cut the rashers into small dice. Put the potato and onion into a basin, add egg, bacon, flour and seasoning. Stir these together until evenly blended. Heat some fat in a frying pan, put dessertspoonsful of the mixture into the fat and fry on both sides until golden brown. Serve hot. (7–8 bites)

## 27. TRADITIONAL CORNISH PASTY

A traditional Cornish Pasty recipe, given to me by Mrs Joyce Rogers of Mylor, Cornwall, who is a Cornish lady.

INGREDIENTS

½ lb. short crust pastry
¼ lb. lean steak (i.e. chuck steak)
2 medium sized potatoes

1 small onion
2 slices turnip
Pepper and salt to taste

METHOD: Make the pastry the day before required, wrap in paper and leave in a cool place.

The following day roll out the pastry into a round 9" in diameter. Peel the vegetables and cut the meat into small pieces. Thinly slice the potatoes on to the pastry, then the turnip and onion, keeping the ingredients towards the centre. On top place the meat and season well.

31

Damp the edge of the pastry with a little cold water, pinch them together and crimp the edge with the fingers. Make a small hole in the top of the pasty, place on a baking tin and bake at approximately 425° F or mark 8 for about 45–55 minutes, then it's ready for serving. To test when done put a skewer in the hole in the top and if all the ingredients feel soft the pasty is done.

All vegetables and the meat must be raw and not cooked for a real Cornish Pasty.

*Dry the potatoes and turnip before slicing into the pasty.*

(1 pasty)

## 28. CHEESE AND MINCE PIE

A dish to make when using up some of the left-overs from a joint of beef, or with fresh mince if you prefer.

INGREDIENTS

½ lb. thinly sliced potatoes
3½ oz. grated Cheddar cheese
½ lb. cooked minced beef
Salt and pepper to taste

Little gravy
¼ pint white sauce (pouring consistency)

METHOD: Into a greased ovenproof dish place half the potatoes in a layer, sprinkle lightly with some of the cheese. Spread the mince on top and cover with the remaining potatoes in a layer. Make up the sauce and put half the remaining cheese into it, then pour over the potatoes. Cover with the remaining cheese and cook at approximately 400° F or mark 6 for about 45 minutes. Serve hot. (2–3 portions)

## 29. SAUSAGE AND EGG ROLL

This can be eaten at home or on a picnic depending on the weather forecast for the day.

INGREDIENTS

*Cheese pastry*

6 oz. plain flour
Pinch salt

3 oz. grated Cheddar cheese
1 large egg yolk

Pinch Cayenne pepper    Little water to mix
3 oz. butter

*Filling*

1 lb. pork sausage meat    Little milk for glazing
4 standard hard-boiled eggs

METHOD: Sieve the flour, salt and pepper into a basin then rub in the butter until it resembles fine breadcrumbs, mix in the cheese until evenly blended then mix to a fairly stiff dough with the egg yolk and water.

Roll the cheese pastry out on a lightly floured board into an oblong approximately 11″ × 8″. Flatten the sausage meat into an oblong slightly smaller than the pastry, place the shelled eggs down the centre and form into a roll. Place the sausage roll on one side of the pastry and roll up as for sausage rolls, damping the edges first. Seal well, glaze all over with a little milk, place on a baking sheet and bake at approximately 400° F or mark 6 for 30 minutes then reduce the temperature to approximately 375° F or mark 4–5 for a further 30 minutes. Eat either hot or cold.    (6 portions)

## 30. GUY FAWKES SAUSAGE SIZZLE

INGREDIENTS

$\frac{1}{2}$ lb. chipolata sausages    8 rashers streaky bacon
  (with skins)    $\frac{1}{4}$ lb. button mushrooms

*Sauce*

5 tablespoonsful white    2 level tablespoonsful
  vinegar    Demerara sugar
2 rounded tablespoonsful    1 teaspoonful Worcester
  redcurrant jelly    sauce
1 level tablespoonful ready-
  made mustard

METHOD: Carefully twist the sausages in two, then cut in half. Slightly spread the rashers of bacon with a palatte knife then cut in half. Wrap each half sausage in a piece of bacon, and grill on a medium heat for about 10–15 minutes, turning frequently. Cook the mushrooms at the same time.

While these are cooking prepare the sauce by heating together in a small saucepan all the sauce ingredients. Simmer together, stirring from time to time, until the sauce is of a coating consistency.

Place the cooked sausages and mushrooms on cocktail sticks and serve the sauce separately as a dip.          (16 portions)


## 31. MARROW CARGO

Marrow cooked in this way may well appeal to those who do not like it as a second vegetable.

INGREDIENTS

½ a medium sized marrow
  (cut lengthwise)
Little boiling water
Little melted butter
8-oz. can baked beans

1 teaspoonful Mango chutney
1 level teaspoonful dry
  mustard
Few drops Worcester sauce
½ lb. large pork sausages

METHOD: Preheat the oven to approximately 400° F or mark 6. Peel the half marrow and remove the seeds. Place it in a large baking tin or dish, which will hold water. Pour in sufficient boiling water to come ½″ up the side of the marrow. Lightly brush the cut edge of the marrow with the melted butter, place in the oven and bake for 30 minutes.

In the meantime, mix together the beans, mustard, sauce and chutney. Divide each sausage into two by twisting them in the middle, and cut through the skin. After the 30 minutes fill the marrow half with the bean mixture and lay the sausages on the top. Return the dish to the oven and bake a further 30 minutes or until the marrow is tender and the sausages brown. Serve at once.          (3–4 portions)

# Meat

### 32. STUFFED BREAST OF LAMB

Apricots and breast of lamb give an unusual but tasty flavour to this dish.

INGREDIENTS

1 breast of lamb approx.
 1½ lb.

*Stuffing*

12 oz. canned apricots
 (drained)
 *or*
12 oz. dried apricots (cooked
 and drained)

4 oz. sausage meat
8 oz. fresh breadcrumbs
Salt and pepper

METHOD: Bone the breast of lamb, or get your butcher to do it for you. Mash the apricots in a basin with the sausage meat and breadcrumbs, season to taste. Spread the stuffing on the inner side of the lamb, roll up loosely and tie with thin string in several places to keep it in a neat shape. Place the joint in the roasting pan and roast at approx. 350° F or mark 4 for approx. 1 hour. Baste with a little bone stock during cooking if desired. (3–4 portions)

## 33. SWEET AND SOUR PORK

Pork done this way makes a tasty dish and gives variation to the family meals.

INGREDIENTS

¾ lb. lean pork (fore end)
2 level dessertspoonsful
    clear honey
1 tablespoonful malt vinegar
1 tablespoonful dry sherry

1 tablespoonful soy sauce
⅛ pint beef stock
½ clove garlic (crushed)
¼ oz. cornflour

METHOD: Trim any surplus fat from the meat and cut into ½″ cubes. In a basin mix together honey, vinegar, sherry, soy sauce, stock and garlic. Add the pork and marinate it for several hours or overnight. Lightly grease an ovenproof casserole and pour the meat and marinade into it, cover with a well-fitting lid and cook at approximately 350° F or mark 3–4 for about 1¼ hours or until the meat is tender. When cooked strain off the liquid. Mix the cornflour with a little of the liquid to form a paste and then add the remaining liquid. Bring this to the boil, stirring until it thickens, pour over the meat and serve hot with some cooked rice.                    (2–3 portions)


## 34. STUFFED STREAKY PORK

Roast streaky pork is good to eat and makes a hot or cold meal when you have to watch the purse strings.

INGREDIENTS

2½ lb. raw boned and scored
    streaky pork
4 oz. raw pork sausage meat
2 oz. fresh white breadcrumbs
1 small onion (finely chopped)
¼ teaspoonful dried sage

¼ teaspoonful dried thyme
1 level dessertspoonful
    chopped parsley
Pepper and salt
1 small egg

METHOD: Wipe the joint with a clean damp cloth, spread some ready-mixed English mustard on the inside of the meat. Make the stuffing by mixing together all the remaining ingredients until evenly blended, then spread over the joint on top of the mustard. Roll the joint up and secure well with string. Rub the scored rind with some common block salt so that it gets well into the score marks. Place in a roasting pan and roast at approximately 400° F or mark 6 for about 2 hours. Serve either hot or cold.

## 35. SPICED TOPSIDE

Here are 3 ways to Pot Roast joints of beef.

INGREDIENTS

| | |
|---|---|
| 4 lb. topside of beef | 1 wineglass red wine |
| Little plain flour ⎱ Seasoned | 1 bay leaf |
| Salt and pepper ⎰ flour | 3 cloves |
| 1 tablespoonful dripping or oil | 1 peeled and sliced onion |
| | ¼ pint stock |

METHOD: Heat the dripping or oil in a casserole, saucepan or oven roaster, deep enough to hold the joint. Dust the meat lightly with the seasoned flour and brown the meat well *all over* in the hot fat. Pour off any surplus fat then add the remaining ingredients. Cover the saucepan firmly with a lid and *simmer very gently* allowing 35–45 minutes to the lb. When using a casserole or oven roaster cover and cook at approximately 325° F or mark 2 allowing 35–45 minutes to the lb. When cooked dish up the meat, remove any fat from the gravy and strain if desired. If liked, vegetables such as carrots, onions and potatoes may be added approximately 1 hour before the cooking time is completed, depending on the size.

INGREDIENTS *for Brisket*

| | |
|---|---|
| 3–4 lb. brisket of beef | 8 fluid oz. stock |
| Seasoned flour | ½ packet onion soup |
| 1 tablespoonful dripping or oil | |

INGREDIENTS *for Shoulder*

| | |
|---|---|
| 2 lb. shoulder of beef | 1 tablespoonful dripping or oil |
| Seasoned flour | ⅛ pint stock |

37

METHOD: Use the instructions as given above for cooking both of these joints. (6–8 portions)

## 36. BACON COUNTRY STYLE

Can be re-wrapped in foil when cold and taken on a picnic.

INGREDIENTS

4 lb. joint of collar bacon
¼ pint cider

1 large orange (grated rind and juice)

METHOD: Soak the joint in cold water overnight. Carefully remove the skin with a sharp knife. Lay the bacon on a piece of foil large enough to wrap it completely and place in a roasting pan. Turn the sides of the foil up, sprinkle with rind and juice of the orange and pour over the cider. Fold over the ends of the foil to form a parcel and press it together just to hold it in place. Bake at approximately 400° F or mark 6 allowing 25 minutes to the lb. or approximately 2 hours cooking all together. Open up the foil when cooked and allow to become cold before carving. Serve with salad in season or hot vegetables and potatoes.

## 37. BEEF CASSEROLE

Shin of beef is just right for a casserole dish as it has plenty of flavour and gives a good rich gravy.

INGREDIENTS

1 oz. butter
1½ lb. shin of beef (cut into cubes)
10½-oz. can condensed cream of celery soup
¼ pint water

4 oz. mushrooms (sliced)
1 large onion (sliced)
1 rounded tablespoonful chopped gherkins or sour cucumbers

METHOD: Melt the butter in a frying pan, and fry the beef gently for about 3 minutes. Put it into an ovenproof casserole and add all remaining ingredients. Cover with a lid and bake at approximately 350° F or mark 3 for about 2 hours or until the meat is tender. (4–6 portions)

## 38. BARLEY LAMB

This dish uses one of the cheaper cuts of lamb, and makes a tasty lunch or supper dish.

INGREDIENTS

1 lb. scrag end of neck of lamb
1 oz. butter or margarine
1 medium sized onion (peeled and thinly sliced)
1½ oz. seasoned flour
¾ pint stock

1 large carrot (peeled and thinly sliced)
¾ oz. pearl barley
1 large potato (peeled and thinly sliced)
Little chopped parsley
Little black pepper } Garnish

METHOD: Trim the meat and remove any excess fat, cut into even sized pieces if necessary, then dip in seasoned flour. In a frying pan melt the butter or margarine and fry the meat for about 5 minutes or until brown all over. Put the meat into a deep ovenproof casserole and fry the onion golden brown. Add these to the casserole. Add the remaining seasoned flour to the frying pan, stir and cook for about 2–3 minutes, remove the pan from the heat and gradually add the stock, stirring all the time to ensure a smooth sauce. Return the pan to the heat and bring to the boil, cook for 1 minute then remove the pan from the heat and add the carrots and pearl barley. Stir all together then pour into the casserole. Arrange the potatoes on the top, cover with a lid and bake at approximately 325° F or mark 2 for 2–2½ hours. Remove the lid for the last 30 minutes cooking to brown the potatoes. Serve hot sprinkled with the parsley and black pepper. (3–4 portions)

Here are three different ways of cooking gammon joints for Christmas. The joints used are middle gammon, hock and gammon slipper.

## 39. CHRISTMAS PARTY GAMMON

INGREDIENTS

4–5-lb. joint middle gammon    Approx. 12 cloves

1 sachet bouquet garni
4 oz. Demerara sugar

Large can halved peaches

*Cranberry sauce*

½ lb. fresh cranberries
6 oz. castor sugar

¼ pint water

METHOD: Soak the joint overnight. Put the joint into a large saucepan with the bouquet garni, and cover the joint with water. Bring slowly to almost boiling point, then reduce the heat to *simmering* point and simmer 25 minutes to the lb. When cooked take the joint from the saucepan, remove the skin and place in a piece of foil in a roasting pan. Score the fat diagonally, sprinkle on a little of the peach juice and press the sugar well into the fat. Stud each diamond with a clove and bake at approximately 450° F or mark 8–9 for 15 minutes. Serve cold with the peaches and cranberry sauce.

*To make the sauce:* Heat the sugar and water together in a pan and stir until the sugar has dissolved. Add the cranberries and cook gently for about 10 minutes when the skins should be soft. Allow the sauce to become quite cold before serving in the hollows of the peaches. Any remaining sauce can be served in a sauce boat.

## 40. GAMMON HOCK WITH ORANGE

INGREDIENTS

1 gammon hock (approximately 2½ lb. in weight)

2 oz. Demerara sugar
3 large oranges

METHOD: Prepare and cook as for the Christmas Party Gammon, then place in foil in a roasting pan. Score the fat diagonally, mix 1 dessertspoonful of orange juice with the sugar and spread over the fat. Pour any remaining juice from 1 orange into the foil, and baste during the following cooking period. Bake at approximately 450° F or mark 8–9 for 15 minutes. Serve cold with slices of orange cut from the remaining 2 oranges, which have had the rind removed.

## 41. CRANBERRY GLAZED GAMMON SLIPPER

INGREDIENTS

1 gammon slipper (approximately 1½ lb. in weight)

2 tablespoonsful cranberry
  sauce

METHOD: Prepare and cook as for the Christmas Party Gammon, then place in foil in a small roasting pan. Spoon the
cranberry sauce over the fat part of the joint and bake at
approximately 450° F or mark 8–9 for 15 minutes. Serve cold.


## 42. PRUNE STUFFED LOIN OF PORK

An unusual combination, but one I hope you will like.

INGREDIENTS

1½-lb. loin of pork
4–5 prunes (uncooked)
1 teaspoonful salt

½ teaspoonful pepper
½ pint bone stock

METHOD: Rinse the prunes in warm water, cut in half and remove the stones. Remove the rind and any excess fat from the
joint, then wipe with a clean damp cloth. Make two 1″ deep
cuts lengthwise in the loin on the fat side. Insert the halved
prunes one at a time with the cut side down into the slits. Tie
the meat securely in several places with string, and rub a little
salt and pepper into the meat. Place the joint in a roasting pan
fat side up and roast at approx. 350° F or mark 4 for about
1¼ hours, basting the joint occasionally with the bone stock
which has been put into the pan.                    (4 portions)


## 43. DEVILLED TROTTERS

A very reasonable and tasty meal.

INGREDIENTS

4 large pig's trotters
1 medium sized onion
1 bay leaf
Small quantity melted lard

Creamed potatoes for 4
  portions
Salt and Cayenne pepper

METHOD: Get the butcher to split the trotters for you, then wash them well in cold water. Put the trotters into a saucepan and cover them with water, add the onion cut into four, also the bay leaf and simmer until tender. Skim the surface of the water from time to time to keep the stock clear. When cooked remove them from the pan and drain well. Place them on a grill pan, skin side up, brush over with the melted lard, and sprinkle with a little Cayenne pepper and salt. Grill until golden brown and serve on a dish of hot creamed potatoes.

(4 portions)


## 44. ROAST SPARE RIBS WITH SPICY SAUCE

The spicy sauce makes all the difference to the Roast Spare Ribs.

INGREDIENTS

2 lb. pork spare ribs
Salt and black pepper to taste
1 can condensed tomato soup
2 teaspoonsful Worcester
  sauce
1 clove of garlic, crushed
  (optional)

1 teaspoonful malt vinegar
1 teaspoonful mixed dried
  herbs
Grilled bacon rolls ⎱ For
       or            ⎰ garnish
Fried bacon rinds
1 piece of foil 18″ × 18″

METHOD: Place the foil on a baking tin, put the ribs in the centre, and season with salt and pepper. Bring the sides and ends of the foil up to overlap, making a loose parcel. Roast at approx. 450° F or mark 8 for about 50 minutes. Then open the foil and cook for a further 20 minutes at the same temperature to brown the joint.

In the meantime, make the sauce. In a small saucepan pour the soup, add Worcester sauce, garlic, vinegar and herbs. Simmer gently for 5 minutes with the lid on the pan. Serve with the ribs and garnish with the bacon.          (4–6 portions)

# Fish

## 45. HOT SAVOURY CRAB

This makes a change from cold Dressed Crab, and is delicious for those who like a cheesy flavour.

INGREDIENTS

6 oz. fresh crab meat (from the shell)
1½ oz. fresh white breadcrumbs
3 oz. grated Cheddar cheese
¼ teaspoonful Cayenne pepper

¼ teaspoonful Worcester sauce
¼ teaspoonful salt
Pinch dry mustard
2 tablespoonsful single cream

METHOD: Put the crab meat into a basin, add breadcrumbs, cheese, pepper, mustard and salt. Stir together then add the sauce and sufficient cream to bind into a fairly soft consistency. Put the mixture into a greased ovenproof dish and bake at approximately 400° F or mark 6 for about 20 minutes. Serve with new potatoes and/or a salad.                    (2 portions)

## 46. CREAMED HADDOCK

To ring the changes try this made with smoked cod instead of haddock.

INGREDIENTS

| | |
|---|---|
| 1 oz. margarine | 1 lb. smoked haddock |
| 1 oz. plain flour | (cooked and flaked) |
| ¾ pint milk | 2 standard hard-boiled eggs |
| 3 oz. grated Cheddar cheese | (chopped) |
| | Pepper to taste |

METHOD: In a saucepan melt the margarine, stir in the flour and cook for 2–3 minutes. Remove the pan from the heat and gradually add the milk, beating well all the time. When all added bring the sauce to the boil, stirring all the time and cook until it thickens. Stir in the fish, cheese and eggs in this order. Re-heat until almost boiling, pour into a hot ovenproof dish, sprinkle on the remaining cheese and brown under the grill. Serve very hot. (4–5 portions)

## 47. KIPPER IN A JUG

A quick dish to make and useful for those in bed-sitters.

INGREDIENTS

| | |
|---|---|
| 1 fresh kipper | 2 small pats butter |
| Boiling water | |

METHOD: Remove the head and wash the kipper, then push a metal skewer through the thick part of the tail. Rest the skewer on the top of a tall jug, deep enough to hold the kipper, and pour in the boiling water right up to the top. Remove the kipper after 5 minutes when it will be cooked. Serve with the pats of butter. (1 portion)

## 48. CRUNCHY TOPPED HERRINGS

Served with grilled tomatoes which have been cut in half and seasoned with salt, pepper and a little sugar, this makes a tasty meal.

3 large herrings
3 teaspoonsful ready-made
  mild mustard
1 teaspoonful castor sugar

3 drops vinegar
Salt and pepper to taste
3 tomatoes

*Topping*

1½ oz. fresh white
  breadcrumbs

1½ oz. melted butter

METHOD: Scale, clean and bone the herrings. In a basin mix the mustard, sugar, vinegar, salt and pepper, and when evenly blended spread on the inside of the fillets. Fold each fillet over so that the mustard is on the inside, and place in a greased grill pan or ovenproof dish.

Melt the butter and add the breadcrumbs, and when all the butter has been absorbed, sprinkle over the fish fillets. Grill under a medium heat for about 12 minutes then turn it up high to brown the crumbs.     (3 portions)

## 49. COD FILLETS WITH ORANGE

Cod cooked in this way lifts it out of the ordinary everyday fish, but at the same time still makes a reasonably priced meal.

INGREDIENTS

¾ lb. fresh cod fillet
2 oz. fresh brown
  breadcrumbs
2 oz. butter

1 crushed clove of garlic
  (optional)
1 large orange (rind and juice)
Salt and pepper

METHOD: Melt the butter in a small frying pan, add the breadcrumbs, orange rind and garlic if desired. Stir until all the butter has been absorbed.

Divide the cod fillet into portions, place in a buttered ovenproof dish, and season well with salt and pepper. Cover the fillets with the breadcrumbs, pour over the orange juice, and bake uncovered at approximately 375° F or mark 4–5 for 20–30 minutes depending on the thickness of the fillets. Serve with new potatoes and a watercress salad.     (3 portions)

## 50. KIPPER RAMEKINS

These must be eaten straight from the oven, as they have a soufflé-like texture.

INGREDIENTS

8-oz. packet kipper fillets
1 oz. butter
$\frac{1}{2}$ oz. plain flour
$\frac{1}{4}$ pint milk

2 standard eggs (separated)
1 oz. grated cheese
Salt and pepper
Pinch dry mustard

METHOD: Cook the kippers according to the instructions on the packet. When cooked remove the skin and mash with a fork, retaining any juices from the cooking. In a saucepan melt the butter, add the flour and cook together for 1 minute. Remove the pan from the heat and gradually add the milk to give a smooth sauce. Return the pan to the heat, bring to the boil, stirring all the time, until it thickens. Remove the pan from the heat and add kipper, egg yolks only, cheese, seasoning and mustard. Whip the egg whites stiffly then fold in to the kipper mixture.

Turn the mixture into 5 small greased ovenproof dishes (about $\frac{1}{4}$ pint size) and bake at approximately 425° F or mark 8 for about 15–20 minutes until well risen and golden brown. Serve immediately.                                    (5 portions)


## 51. STUFFED COD CUTLETS

Very few bones to cope with here, as the main ones are removed before cooking. A tasty mid-week dish.

INGREDIENTS

4 cod cutlets
Salt and pepper
Juice of $\frac{1}{2}$ a lemon
1 small onion (chopped)
$\frac{1}{2}$ oz. butter
1 oz. fresh white
  breadcrumbs

$\frac{1}{4}$ teaspoonful tarragon or
  thyme
1 dessertspoonful milk
$\frac{1}{2}$ pint prawn, cheese or
  parsley sauce

46

METHOD: Place the cutlets into a greased ovenproof dish, having first removed the centre bone with a sharp knife. Season with salt and pepper and sprinkle with a few drops of lemon juice. In a small frying pan melt the butter and cook the onion until soft and transparent, then add the breadcrumbs, tarragon or thyme, milk, salt and pepper and remaining lemon juice. Form the mixture into four portions and place in the centre of each cutlet.

Cover the dish with a lid and bake at approximately 375° F or mark 4–5 for about 20 minutes.

During the latter part of the cooking time make up the sauce, and serve poured over the fish or separately in a sauce boat.

(4 portions)

## 52. HERRINGS IN PIQUANT SAUCE

Yet another recipe for herrings – a favourite fish of mine. The piquant sauce gives these fish a lovely flavour, and it's so easy to make.

INGREDIENTS

| | |
|---|---|
| 4 large fresh herrings | Little pepper |
| ½ oz. butter | |

*Sauce*

| | |
|---|---|
| 1 oz. butter | 1 rounded teaspoonful mild |
| 1 medium sized onion | made mustard |
| (chopped) | 1 level teaspoonful salt |
| 1 level tablespoonful black | 1 level teaspoonful paprika |
| treacle | 2¼-oz. can tomato purée |
| 1 tablespoonful malt vinegar | ¼ pint water |

METHOD: Scale, clean, wash and dry the herrings, then place in a greased ovenproof dish. Dot with the ½ oz. butter and season with pepper. Bake at approximately 350° F or mark 3–4 for 15 minutes.

In the meantime make the sauce by lightly frying the onion in butter. Add all the remaining ingredients for the sauce, and when evenly blended, bring to the boil. Pour the sauce over the herrings and return the dish to the oven for a further 15–20 minutes, covered with a piece of foil, and using the same oven temperature. Serve very hot with creamy mashed potatoes.

(4 portions)

## 53. PRAWN AND ASPARAGUS FLAN

When friends are coming in for a meal this recipe makes a tasty dish. It can be eaten cold but I prefer it hot.

### INGREDIENTS

8 oz. short crust pastry
10½-oz. can green asparagus
  spears
½ lb. small prawns or scampi

1 oz. butter
1 oz. plain flour
½ pint milk
Salt and pepper to taste

METHOD: Cut each asparagus spear into 3, then drain well in a colander. If using frozen or canned fish, thaw out and then drain well.

Make a white sauce with the butter, flour, milk and seasoning and when it has thickened and come to the boil, gently stir in the prawns or scampi and asparagus.

Roll out the pastry and line a 9″ flan ring which has been placed on a baking tin. Pour the contents of the saucepan into the flan case and bake at approximately 400° F or mark 6–7 for about 40 minutes. Serve hot. (6 portions)

# Fowl

## 54. PLAIN OR PARTY CHICKEN

Here are two ways of serving the same dish; the difference is in the presentation of the dishes.

INGREDIENTS

2 chicken quarters
1½ oz. butter
1 teaspoonful grated lemon rind
1 tablespoonful fresh lemon juice

¼ pint white wine or water
1 rounded dessertspoonful chopped parsley
Salt and pepper to taste

*Plain garnish*

Few sprigs watercress

*Party garnish*

2–4 slices pineapple

1 oz. blanched and sliced almonds

METHOD: Either cut the chicken quarters in half or leave whole as desired. In a frying pan melt the butter and fry the chicken joints slowly on both sides until golden brown. Allow about 5 minutes on each side.

Put the joints into an ovenproof casserole, add rind, juice, wine or water, parsley and salt and pepper. Cover with a lid and cook at approximately 350° F or mark 3–4 for about 45 minutes or until the joints are tender.

*To serve:* Place the joints on to a hot serving dish, and keep hot while thickening the casserole juices. Garnish with watercress.

*To serve for a party:* Just before the joints are cooked brown the almonds in a little butter, and brush the pineapple with butter and heat through. Serve pineapple rings round the joints, almonds sprinkled over the top and the casserole juices poured over the joints. Garnish with parsley.          (2–4 portions)

## 55. CHICKEN CASSEROLE

A jolly tasty casserole which can be made during most months of the year. You can also keep it hot for people who arrive home late!

INGREDIENTS

2 chicken quarters
1½ oz. butter
1 small onion (finely
  chopped)
2 oz. mushrooms
2 rashers streaky bacon
  (cut into strips)

½ oz. plain flour
Pepper to taste
½ pint chicken stock
3 small tomatoes
  (skinned and quartered)

METHOD: Either cut the chicken quarters in half or leave whole as desired. In a frying pan melt the butter and fry the chicken joints slowly on both sides until golden brown. Allow about 5 minutes on each side.

Put the joints into an ovenproof casserole, add to the remaining butter in the frying pan the onion, mushrooms cut into halves and bacon. Cook gently together for a few minutes. In the meantime blend the flour and pepper with the stock, then add this to the pan, bringing to the boil in order that it may thicken. Finally add the tomatoes and then pour contents of the pan into the casserole. Cover with a lid and cook at approximately 350° F or mark 3–4 for about 45 minutes or until the joints are tender. Garnish with a little chopped parsley if desired.

(2–4 portions)

## 56. CHICKEN SOUP

A delicious and nourishing soup made from a chicken soup pack.

### INGREDIENTS

1 chicken soup pack
Cold water
1 medium sized onion
  (coarsely chopped)

1 carrot (coarsely chopped)
1 bouquet garni
Salt and pepper to taste
1 oz. butter

METHOD: Melt the butter in a frying pan, add the giblets and backbones and fry slowly until lightly browned. Put all joints into a deep saucepan or ovenproof dish, add sufficient cold water to cover (approximately 2 pints), the vegetables and bouquet garni. Cover with a lid and simmer very gently until the meat and giblets are tender. Remove the meat from the bones and cut into small pieces, also the giblets if you like them. Skim the top of the liquid to remove any fat, add the meat to the liquid, adjust seasoning and add a little cooked vermicelli if desired. Serve very hot with crusty bread.

(2–3 portions)


## 57. CURRIED DUCKLING

This recipe makes a duckling soup pack into a meal.

### INGREDIENTS

1 duckling soup pack
3 dessertspoonsful vegetable
  oil
1 medium sized onion
  (chopped)
Small piece root ginger
  (crushed)
1½ level teaspoonsful salt
½ level teaspoonful turmeric
½ level teaspoonful chilli
  powder

½ level teaspoonful garam
  masala
¼ pint stock
2 tomatoes (peeled and
  sliced)
2 tablespoonsful natural
  yoghurt
Hot boiled rice for two
  people

METHOD: Gently simmer the giblets in water until tender to make the stock. Cut the backbone of the duckling into 3 pieces. In a large frying pan heat the oil and fry the onion, and ginger for a few minutes, then add salt, turmeric, garam masala and chilli powder. Stir all well together and cook for 1 minute. Add the drained duckling and fry 4–5 minutes, finally adding the stock.

Cover the pan with a well-fitting lid and simmer for about ½ hour until the duckling is tender. Add the tomatoes and yoghurt and simmer a further 20 minutes with the lid on or off depending on whether you want a thick or thin sauce. Serve with hot boiled rice and some or all of the suggested side dishes. (2 portions)

*Suggested side dishes:*

1. Diced fresh grapefruit
2. Finely diced tomatoes
3. Finely chopped peanuts
4. Whole peanuts
5. Desiccated coconut
6. Diced banana
7. Mango chutney

## 58. CHICKEN AND POTATO NUGGETS

I made this with half of a chicken quarter, and therefore had two meals almost for the price of one.

INGREDIENTS

2 oz. diced and cooked chicken
4 oz. cold mashed potato
Salt and pepper to taste

1 small egg
Small quantity crushed cornflakes
Fat for deep fat frying

METHOD: In a basin mix together the chicken and potato, until evenly blended, seasoning to taste. Form into 8 or 10 balls, coat in beaten egg and cornflakes. Place them into the hot fat and fry until golden brown and thoroughly heated through – about 5–7 minutes. Drain on absorbent paper and serve at once. (8–10 nuggets)

## 59. CHICKEN FOR ONE

If you live alone, here's a dish just for you.

INGREDIENTS

1 chicken quarter
½ lemon
Salt
1 oz. butter

2 teaspoonsful vegetable oil
1 rasher streaky bacon
  (chopped)
2 oz. mushrooms (sliced)

METHOD: Rub the joint with lemon and sprinkle with salt. Heat the butter and oil in a grill pan which has had the grid removed. Lay the chicken skin side down in the pan, brush all over with melted butter, and cook in the lowest position of the grill, on a medium heat for 15 minutes. Turn the joint over, brush with the fat in the pan, add the bacon and mushrooms, turning them also in the fat. Continue cooking slowly for another 10 to 15 minutes, brushing with the pan juices from time to time, until cooked through and golden brown. Put the joint on to a hot serving dish or plate, add a squeeze of lemon juice to the pan, mix well together and pour over the chicken. Serve with potato crisps or mashed potatoes and watercress.                                    (1 portion)


## 60. CHICKEN, CELERY AND APPLE SALAD

A crisp salad using up the left-over chicken.

INGREDIENTS

4 level tablespoonsful
  mayonnaise
4 level tablespoonsful top of
  the milk
Approx. ½ level teaspoonful
  salt
2 large dessert apples
  (cored and cut into dice)

4–5 sticks celery (sliced)
8 oz. cooked chicken
  (cut into dice)
Little finely chopped walnut
1 large tomato
Few lettuce leaves

METHOD: In a large basin mix together the mayonnaise, top of the milk and salt. Add the apple, celery and chicken and stir until evenly blended. If possible allow the mixture to stand in a cool place for about an hour, as this will allow the flavours to blend together.

Arrange the lettuce on a serving dish, pile the mixture in the centre, sprinkle with the chopped walnuts and garnish with tomato.                                                    (3–4 portions)

# Puddings (hot)

## 61. CHOCOLATE ORANGE PUDDING

Chocolate and orange go particularly well together. I like both so this is a favourite pudding of mine.

INGREDIENTS

4 oz. chocolate dots
1 oz. cornflour
1 pint milk

2 oz. castor sugar
1 large or 2 small oranges
3 standard egg yolks

*Topping*

3 standard egg whites

1 level tablespoonful castor sugar

METHOD: Melt the chocolate dots in a basin over a pan of hot but not boiling water. Grate the rind from the orange and cut the orange into thin slices, trimming off the rind with a pair of kitchen scissors.

Blend the cornflour with a little of the cold milk, bring the remainder to the boil and then pour on to the cornflour, add the melted chocolate and return all to the saucepan. Add the 2 oz. of sugar and the grated orange rind, and stir until thick. Cool slightly, add the lightly beaten egg yolks and cook *without boiling* for 10 minutes. Pour into an ovenproof dish.

Arrange the orange slices on top of the chocolate mixture. Whip the egg whites until stiff then fold in the castor sugar, pile on top of the pudding and bake at approximately 375° F or mark 4–5 for 10–15 minutes when the top should be golden brown. Serve at once. (4 portions)

## 62. BAKED APPLE AND LEMON PUDDING

I like a baked suet pudding for a change as the top is crisp unlike a boiled or steamed one, which some people find rather indigestible.

**INGREDIENTS**

8 oz. self-raising flour
4 oz. packaged suet
Pinch salt
Approx. $\frac{1}{4}$ pint milk
2 oz. butter

4 oz. dark soft brown sugar
1$\frac{1}{4}$ lb. Bramley cooking
  apples
Grated rind of 1 lemon
Juice of 2 lemons

METHOD: Grease a 2-pint size pudding basin. In a smaller basin cream together the butter and 2 oz. of the sugar until creamy then put it into the greased basin. To make the pastry, sieve the flour and salt together, add the suet and mix to a firm paste with the milk. Cut off one-third of the pastry and put to one side, then roll out the remaining pastry and line the 2-pint basin. Fill the basin with the peeled, cored and sliced apples, sprinkling with sugar and lemon juice and rind alternately. Roll out the remaining pastry to form a lid, damp the edge and press well into position on top of the fruit. Bake on a baking sheet at approximately 400° F or mark 6 for 15 minutes and then reduce the heat to approximately 325° F or mark 2 for a further hour. Serve either from the basin or turn out upside down on a hot serving dish.                 (4–6 portions)


## 63. GOOSEBERRY AND STRAWBERRY PIE

A lot of people do not like gooseberries on their own but mixed with strawberries they make a delicious pie.

**INGREDIENTS**

12 oz. fresh English
  gooseberries
6 oz. fresh English strawberries

Castor sugar to taste
4 oz. rough puff pastry

METHOD: Prepare the fruit then cook *very slowly* with 1 table-spoonful of cold water, until almost tender. Put a little of the fruit into an ovenproof dish, sprinkle with castor sugar, and continue in layers until all the fruit has been used. Roll out the pastry into a lid, place on top of the fruit, flute the edge and make a slit for the steam to escape. Bake at approximately 450° F or mark 8–9 for about 30 minutes. When the pastry is golden brown remove from the oven and sprinkle with castor sugar. Delicious served with cream. (4–6 portions)

## 64. AUNTIE MAUD'S PUMPKIN PIE

This recipe was given to me by a friend who lives in the village of Pirton in Hertfordshire.

INGREDIENTS

| | |
|---|---|
| 6 oz. Demerara sugar | 12 oz. cooked pumpkin |
| 1 oz. seedless raisins | 1 level teaspoonful mixed |
| 1 oz. sultanas | spice |
| 1 oz. currants | 2 standard eggs |
| 1 oz. chopped candied peel | 1 tablespoonful rum |
| 1 oz. chopped almonds or walnuts | ¼ teaspoonful salt |

METHOD: In a basin mix together the sugar, salt, spice and fruit, then add the cooked pumpkin, and blend well together.

Beat the yolks of the two eggs and the white of one together and stir into the pumpkin mixture. Beat the remaining egg white until stiff and fold in, finally adding the rum. When evenly blended pour into a pie dish lined with short crust partry, cover with a pastry lid and bake at approximately 300° F or mark 1–2 for about 45 minutes to 1 hour. Serve hot. (6 portions)

## 65. OLD-FASHIONED RHUBARB PUDDING

This is just the pudding for a really cold day, and I first tried it just after all the rich Xmas fare!

INGREDIENTS

1 oz. butter
1½ oz. Demerara sugar

8 oz. suet crust pastry

*Filling*

1 lb. trimmed and thinly
sliced early rhubarb
1 oz. chopped candied peel
2 oz. currants
Grated rind and juice of
½ lemon

Approximately 4 oz. castor
sugar
Small pinch cinnamon
Approx. ½ teacupful water

METHOD: Use the 1 oz. of butter to coat thickly the inside of a 2-pint pudding basin, add the demerara sugar and turn the basin round until it is coated. Line the basin with two-thirds of the pastry, rolling out the remaining one-third for the lid. Put the following ingredients into the basin in layers: rhubarb, peel, currants, rind and juice of lemon and sugar to taste, finally adding the cinnamon and water. Cover with the suet crust lid, seal well and cover with a piece of greased greaseproof paper. Bake at approximately 350° F or mark 3–4 for 1¼–1½ hours, depending how thinly you cut the rhubarb. Serve either turned out on to a dish or in the basin itself.          (6 portions)

## 66. CRUNCHY FRUIT PUDDING

The fruits can be varied according to the season, as the topping goes very well with most fruits.

INGREDIENTS

½ lb. cooking apples
¼ lb. plums

Sugar to taste

*Topping*

2 oz. butter
3 oz. dark brown sugar
(pieces)

2 oz. cornflakes (slightly
crushed)

METHOD: Peel, core and slice the apples, then cook without water but with sugar to taste until tender. Stone the plums and cook with sugar only, then drain off excess syrup. Put the plums into an ovenproof dish, add the apple on the top.

In a saucepan melt the butter and sugar, add the cornflakes and stir until they are well coated with the syrup. Place this mixture on top of the fruit and bake in an oven at approximately 350° F or mark 3 for 20–25 minutes. Serve at once with cream if liked. (3 portions)

## 67. APPLE SYRUP PUDDING

This recipe was given to me by a regular viewer living in Little Oxhey, Watford. It is a delicious pudding.

INGREDIENTS

2 large eggs, their weight in self-raising flour, butter and castor sugar
2 medium sized cooking apples (peeled, cored and chopped)

1 dessertspoonful fresh lemon juice
4 level tablespoonsful golden syrup

METHOD: Well grease with butter a 2-pint pie dish, and put 2 tablespoonsful of syrup in the base. Cream the butter and sugar until light and fluffy, add remaining syrup and beat well. Next add 1 tablespoonful of flour and the beaten eggs and beat again. Fold in lightly the remaining flour, apples and lemon juice. When evenly blended turn into the prepared pie dish, level the top and cover with a well-greased paper.

Stand the pie dish in an ovenproof dish containing some hot water and bake at approximately 350° F or mark 3–4 for about 1½ hours. Serve hot. (6 portions)
N.B. If using half the amount of mixture allow about 45 minutes at the same temperature.

## 68. RHUBARB AND HONEY PUDDING

This is a lovely pudding for those who like a taste of honey with rhubarb, and it takes very little time to prepare.

INGREDIENTS

*Base*

¾ lb. trimmed rhubarb (cut in thin slices)
4 oz. castor sugar

2 tablespoonsful cold water
Small pinch salt

*Topping*

2 oz. melted butter
5 level tablespoonsful clear honey

½ level teaspoonful ground nutmeg
4 thin slices bread from a 2-lb. loaf

METHOD: Lightly grease a 2-pint ovenproof pie dish, add the ingredients for the base of the pudding and combine well together. In a 2-pint basin blend together the butter, honey, nutmeg and bread cut into 1″ squares, until all the bread is covered with the mixture. Arrange these ingredients on top of the rhubarb, place the pie dish on to a baking tin and bake at approximately 375° F or mark 4–5 for 30–35 minutes, or until the topping is crisp and golden brown and the rhubarb cooked.

(4 portions)

## 69. APPLE AND MINCEMEAT PUDDING

This dish can be prepared ready for the oven in half an hour or less, providing there are no interruptions!

INGREDIENTS

*Base*

1 lb. Bramley cooking apples
2 oz. sultanas or raisins
Approx. 3 oz. granulated sugar

¼ teaspoonful ground cinnamon
1 teaspoonful fresh lemon juice
1 tablespoonful water

*Topping*

6 oz. self-raising flour
Pinch salt
1 oz. castor sugar
1½ oz. cooking fat or lard

4–5 tablespoonsful milk
Approx. 3 tablespoonsful mincemeat

METHOD: Peel, core and slice the apples and place in a saucepan with the other ingredients for the base, then cook until the apples are tender.

Into a basin sieve the flour, salt and sugar, rub in the cooking fat or lard until the mixture resembles fine breadcrumbs. Mix to a fairly soft dough with the milk. Roll the mixture out into an oblong on a lightly floured board, until it is about $\frac{1}{8}''$ thick, spread the mincemeat over the dough, dampen the edges and roll up as for a swiss roll. Cut into slices about $\frac{3}{4}''$ thick.

When the apple mixture is cooked place it in the base of a 2-pint dish and arrange the mincemeat slices all over the top. Put the dish on to a baking tin and bake at approximately 425° F or mark 8 for about 25 minutes, or until the top is golden brown. Serve hot with cream, ice cream or custard.

(4–6 portions)

# Puddings (cold)

## 70. NORFOLK SYLLABUB

I made this dessert for a very special occasion, it was enjoyed
by those who tried it so I hope you'll enjoy it as well.

INGREDIENTS

½ pint real double dairy
   cream
Grated rind of 2 lemons
1½ fluid oz. fresh lemon juice
3 oz. castor sugar

1½ fluid oz. whisky
1 oz. finely chopped
   hazelnuts
1 oz. finely grated plain
   chocolate

METHOD: In a basin half whip the cream and sugar together.
Add the lemon juice and whisky alternately *very very slowly*
and whip in with a fork. *Do not overbeat*. If the lemon juice is
added too quickly it may curdle.

    When all the juice and whisky have been added, blend in
the rind, nuts, and chocolate by stirring until evenly blended.

Pile into individual glasses and chill for some hours before serving. Garnish with a small wedge of plain chocolate and/or a small strip of lemon peel. (6–8 portions)

## 71. RASPBERRY MERINGUE PIE

A quick sweet requiring little cooking and therefore a dish to make when you're in a hurry.

INGREDIENTS

6-oz. packet of chocolate chip and nut cookies
15½-oz. can raspberries (drained)

3 large egg whites
2 oz. castor sugar

METHOD: Well drain the raspberries and put into an ovenproof dish. Whip together the egg whites and the sugar until stiff. Crush the cookies finely with a rolling pin, and fold into the egg white mixture. When evenly blended pile on to the fruit, sprinkle the top with a little more castor sugar and bake at approximately 400° F or mark 6 for about 30 minutes, or until the top is crisp and golden. Serve hot. (6 portions)

## 72. STRAWBERRY CREAM ROLL

Serve thinly sliced for tea or in thicker slices as a dessert.

INGREDIENTS

*Roll*  1 large egg
1½ oz. castor sugar

1 oz. self-raising flour

*Filling*  2–3 oz. double cream

2 oz. fresh English strawberries

METHOD: Grease and line a swiss roll tin approximately 11″ × 7″ with greased greaseproof paper. Whisk the egg and sugar together until thick and creamy, so that the beater will leave a trail on top of the mixture when lifted. Fold in the sieved flour until evenly blended and then pour the mixture into the prepared tin, tipping it to ensure an even thickness all over. Bake at approximately 425° F or mark 8 for 9–10 minutes.

Turn the swiss roll out on to a sugared paper, remove the paper from the base, trim the edges with a sharp knife and roll up with the paper inside. When cold, unroll, spread with the whipped cream and cover with the strawberries, roll up again, dredge with castor sugar and serve.           (4–6 portions)


## 73. ORANGE AND LEMON CREAM

A quickly made dessert, for the family or as a party dish.

INGREDIENTS

| | |
|---|---|
| 2–5-oz. cartons soured cream | Juice of ½ lemon |
| 2 large oranges | 1½ oz. castor sugar |
| | 12 sponge biscuit fingers |

METHOD: Put the soured cream into a basin. Cut the biscuits in half. Grate the rind of 1 orange into a basin, and cut a thin slice from the centre of the second orange for decoration. Squeeze the juice from both oranges into the rind, add the sugar, and then stir this mixture into the soured cream. When blended, pour into 4 individual dishes, and when the mixture starts to set place six halved biscuits round the outer edge of each dish. Chill well before serving and decorate with small pieces cut from the remaining slice.           (4 portions)


## 74. STRAWBERRY ALASKA

Here's a variation of the well-known baked Alaska when strawberries are in season.

INGREDIENTS

| | |
|---|---|
| 7″ sponge flan case | 4–6 oz. fresh English strawberries |
| 1 square block vanilla ice cream | |

*Meringue*

| | |
|---|---|
| 3 large egg whites | Small pinch cream of tartar |
| 3 level tablespoonsful castor sugar | |

METHOD: Whisk the egg whites and cream of tartar together until stiff, then carefully fold in the sugar. Place the flan on a heatproof dish, arrange most of the strawberries in the base and place the ice cream on top. Cover *very quickly* with the meringue, and when completely covered over the flan edge put into the oven at approximately 450° F or mark 8–9 for 2–3 minutes. Garnish with remaining strawberries. Serve at once.

(4–6 portions)

## 75. LEMON MERINGUE NESTS

The tangy lemon filling in the meringue makes this one of my favourite party pieces.

INGREDIENTS

*Meringue*

3 large egg whites — 6 oz. castor sugar

*Filling*

3-oz. packet cream cheese spread — Small size can condensed milk
4 fluid oz. fresh lemon juice

METHOD: Whisk the egg whites until stiff, gradually fold or whip in the sugar. Pipe into nest shapes with a large pipe on to greased baking tins and bake very gently at approximately 150° F or mark ¼ for 2–3 hours or until they lift easily from the tins. When cold store in an airtight tin until required.
*To make the filling:* Beat the cheese until soft and smooth, gradually add the condensed milk, and when thoroughly mixed very gradually add the lemon juice. When blended, spoon into the meringue cases and decorate.

(Approx. 6 portions)

## 76. STRAWBERRY AND BANANA MERINGUE

The meringues can be made in advance and used when you're short of time.

INGREDIENTS

*Meringue*

3 large egg whites ⎫ Makes
6 oz. castor sugar ⎬ two 6″
            ⎭ cases

*Filling*

2 bananas
¼ lb. English strawberries

1 dessertspoonful fresh
   orange juice

METHOD: Whip the egg whites until stiff, then fold in the castor sugar. Spread some of the mixture on to well-oiled greaseproof paper, which has been put on a baking tin. Spread the mixture into two 6″ circles, then pipe the remaining mixture round the outer edges to build up the edges. Place in the oven at approximately 200° F or mark ½ for about 2 hours or until the cases have dried out. Fill one case when cold with the following filling and store the other case for use another day.

Save 6 strawberries for decoration, also several slices of banana which should be put into a little orange juice to prevent them going brown. In a basin mash the remaining strawberries and bananas then add the dessertspoonful of orange juice. Mix all well together, then fill the meringue shell just before serving. Decorate with the remaining strawberries and slices of banana.

(4 portions)


## 77. CHOCOLATE AND BANANA TRIFLE

If you have 3 egg yolks left over here is a dessert you can make. It can also be made the day before you eat it.

INGREDIENTS

4 sponge cakes (halved)
Small quantity lemon curd
2 large bananas (sliced)
1 tablespoonful sherry

½ pint milk
3 large egg yolks
4 oz. dark chocolate chips

METHOD: Spread the split sponge cakes with lemon curd. Place half of these lemon curd side up in a glass serving dish. Cover with half of the sliced banana, continue in the same way with another layer, then sprinkle over the sherry. Boil the milk, allow to cool slightly then pour on to the beaten egg yolks, return the ingredients to the pan add the chocolate, and stir over a gentle heat until well blended, but *do not allow to boil*. When the custard has thickened, pour over the ingredients in the dish. When cold decorate with a little double whipped cream if desired. (6 portions)

## 78. STUFFED PEACHES

A good dessert for Boxing Day after all the rich food on Christmas Day, and it uses up any spare mincemeat.

INGREDIENTS

6 fresh peaches                    Little kirsch
Small quantity mincemeat

METHOD: Peel the peaches if desired, then cut each one in half and remove the stone.

Fill the cavities with the mincemeat and trickle the kirsch over each half peach. Serve as soon as possible as the cut edge of the peaches will discolour with keeping. (6 portions)

## 79. BLACKCURRANT FLUFF

Another cool dessert that can be made in advance, to help the busy housewife.

INGREDIENTS

$\frac{1}{2}$ lb. blackcurrants
Approx. 2 oz. castor sugar
  or to taste
$\frac{1}{2}$ oz. powdered gelatine
3 tablespoonsful cold water

$\frac{1}{2}$ pint sweetened apple purée
$\frac{1}{4}$ pint double cream (lightly whipped)
1 egg white (stiffly beaten)

METHOD: Wash and trim the currants, put them into a saucepan with very little water (approx. 3 tablespoonsful), reserving a few for decoration. Simmer until tender then sieve. Sweeten to taste and return to the pan, adding the gelatine which has been softened in the water. Stir all the ingredients over a low heat until the gelatine has dissolved. Stir this mixture into the apple, and cool before adding the egg white and cream. Serve in tall glasses or as you wish, and when set decorate with sugar-coated sprigs of currants. (2–3 portions)

# Dishes from other Countries

## 80. QUICK APPLE DISH (AUSTRIAN)

This is a delicious apple dish sent to me by a viewer, and it's very simple to make.

INGREDIENTS

3 medium sized apples (Bramleys)
2 tablespoonful water
2 tablespoonful white wine
1 rounded tablespoonful granulated sugar

2 large eggs (whites only)
2 oz. castor sugar
3½ oz. finely chopped nuts
Little lemon juice

METHOD: Peel, core and halve the apples, and rub over with lemon juice. Place the apples (cut side down) in a greased ovenproof dish, add water, wine and sprinkle with granulated sugar. Cover with a piece of foil and bake at approximately 400° F or mark 6 for about 30 minutes, when the apples should be cooked but not broken.

In the meantime, whisk the egg whites stiffly, gradually add the castor sugar and nuts while still beating. Place the meringue mixture over the apples and bake at approximately 425° F or mark 8 for about 10 minutes, or just until the meringue has set. Serve in the dish in which they were baked. (3–6 portions)

# OPEN SANDWICHES (DANISH)

Here is a selection of Danish open sandwiches which are ideal for a party but why not try one when you are on your own for lunch.

## 81. OLIVER TWIST

INGREDIENTS

3 slices Danish pork
   luncheon meat
2 cooked prunes (stoned)
1 slice fresh orange

1 tablespoonful horseradish
   cream
Sprig parsley
Small lettuce leaf

METHOD: Well butter a piece of brown bread. Fold and overlap the 3 slices of meat on to the bread. Put the horseradish cream in the centre. Cut the orange slice to the centre and twist over the cream. Place a prune on either side of the twist, and garnish with the parsley and lettuce. (1 portion)

## 82. CHEF'S SPECIAL

INGREDIENTS

3 thin slices Danish gammon
2 tomato twists
1 cucumber twist

Little scrambled egg
Few chopped chives

METHOD: Well butter a piece of white bread. Arrange gammon slices on the bread in a circle. Place the egg in the centre. Place the twists across the egg and garnish with the chives.

(1 portion)

## 83. PICNIC FANCY

INGREDIENTS

1 hard-boiled egg
1 rasher crisp fried streaky
   bacon

1 tomato twist
Small lettuce leaf
Sprig parsley

METHOD: Well butter a piece of brown bread. Place slices of egg on the bread. Put the lettuce leaf one end, and the bacon

down the middle. Twist tomato across the bacon and garnish
with parsley.                                        (1 portion)


## 84. INTERNATIONAL

INGREDIENTS

2 slices Danish ham
1 heaped dessertspoonful
   Russian salad
2 tomato twists

1 cucumber twist
Small lettuce leaf
Sprig parsley

METHOD: Well butter a piece of brown bread. Fold and overlap
the meat on the bread. Put the Russian salad on top, and place
twists across salad. Garnish with lettuce and parsley.
                                                    (1 portion)


## 85. CONTINENTAL

INGREDIENTS

4 thin slices Danish salami
4 thin slices onion rings

Little lettuce
Sprig parsley

METHOD: Well butter a piece of brown bread. Place 3 slices
of salami flat on the bread and make the other into a cone
shape. Place the onion rings on top and garnish with the lettuce
and parsley.                                        (1 portion)


## 86. SHRIMP CRUSH

INGREDIENTS

1½ oz. fresh or canned
   shrimps
Little mayonnaise

1 lemon twist
Small lettuce leaf
Sprig parsley

METHOD: Well butter a piece of white bread, and place a little
mayonnaise down the centre to hold the topping. Arrange the
shrimps on the bread with the lettuce at one corner. Place some
more mayonnaise down the centre and garnish with the
lemon twist and parsley.                            (1 portion)

## NORWEGIAN DISHES

These recipes were shown to commemorate the 20th anniversary of the Xmas Tree given to this country every Xmas by the people of Norway.

## 87. CHRISTMAS RICE PORRIDGE

INGREDIENTS

6 oz. pudding rice
¾ pint boiling water
1½ pints milk
1 oz. butter or margarine

1 teaspoonful salt
2 oz. castor sugar
1 Jordan almond (blanched)

METHOD: Rinse the rice and put it into the boiling water in the top of a double saucepan. Boil until the water has been absorbed, about 10–15 minutes. Add the milk, salt and sugar. Cover with a lid and simmer until the rice is tender, about 45–50 minutes, stirring frequently.

Stir in the butter and add the almond. Serve with milk, fruit or cinnamon sugar. A little single cream can be added if you wish to enrich the porridge. (4 portions)

## 88. TOMATO-HERRING SALAD

INGREDIENTS

1 salted herring (i.e. 2 fillets)
*or*
Can of spiced herring fillets
½ fresh cucumber
16 cocktail onions (drained)

½ small can tomato purée
5 level tablespoonful castor sugar
2 tablespoonsful salad oil

METHOD: Fillet the herring. Cut each fillet in half lengthwise and then into finger-thick slices. Cut the washed cucumber into pieces of similar size. Mix the herring, cucumber and cocktail onions in a bowl.

Blend together the tomato purée, sugar and oil. Pour the dressing over the herring mixture and stir. Cover the bowl and keep the salad chilled in a cold place. The salad is best if prepared the day before it is to be served. It may be kept for several days in a refrigerator. (4 portions)

## 89. NORWEGIAN CREAM CAKE (BLOTKAKE)

*Base*

7″ fatless sponge sandwich

Drained canned fruits or
fruit salad

Fresh fruits, e.g. bananas,
grapes, fresh peaches etc.

Layers of jelly or fruit in
jelly set in cake tin the
same size as the sponge

Apple purée or jam

Whipped double cream
sweetened with castor or
vanilla sugar

Norwegian fruit compote,
e.g. apricot or currant

METHOD: Cut each sponge cake into 2 rounds. Moisten the
sponge layers as they are filled using sugar syrup, flavoured
with liqueur or rum or with syrup from canned fruit.

Coat the cake with whipped cream – using piping tubes if
liked.

Decorate with choice fruits, fresh or canned, walnuts,
desiccated coconut, glacé fruits or roasted almond flakes.

Eat quickly as it is made with fresh cream.

A selection of recipes using Norwegian fish, some of which can
be kept in the storecupboard as it is canned!

## 90. WHOLE COLD SMOKED MACKEREL

INGREDIENTS

1 whole smoked Norwegian
mackerel (approximately
1 lb. weight)

2 hard-boiled eggs (chopped)

½ small cucumber (diced)

2 tablespoonsful chopped
pickled beetroot

*or*

2 tablespoonsful horseradish
and beetroot sauce

½ lb. raw carrots (grated)

¼ small white cabbage (finely
shredded)

Little parsley for garnish

Norwegian flat bread

METHOD: Slice the mackerel into even slices and place down the
centre of a large serving dish. Arrange the eggs, cucumber,
beetroot, carrots and cabbage in neat piles round the edge of
the dish. Garnish with parsley and serve with the flat bread.

(5–6 portions)

## 91. MUSSELS ON SKEWERS

INGREDIENTS

3¼-oz. can Norwegian mussels    3 grilled tomatoes
½ lb. sliced back bacon    Parsley for garnish
1 teacupful of boiled rice

METHOD: Wrap the mussels in a half slice of bacon. Thread on to skewers and grill quickly on all sides until the bacon is crisp. Serve on a bed of hot boiled rice with the grilled tomatoes. Garnish with parsley.      (2–3 portions)


## 92. PARSLEY AND MUSSEL VOL AU VENTS

INGREDIENTS

6 oz. rough puff pastry

*Sauce*

½ pint milk    Few drops fresh lemon juice
1 oz. plain flour    1 level tablespoonful chopped
1 oz. butter       parsley
Salt and pepper    3¾-oz. can Norwegian mussels

METHOD: Roll out the pastry to ¾" thickness and cut into 2½" rounds with a pastry cutter. Using a smaller cutter about 1" in diameter press into the rounds but do not cut right through. Bake at approximately 425° F or mark 8 for about 15–20 minutes. When cooked remove the centres from the cases and fill.

Make the sauce by blending the flour and butter together in a saucepan over a low heat. Gradually add the milk to form a smooth sauce, bring to the boil and add the remaining ingredients. When the sauce comes back to the boil remove from the heat and fill the cases.      (8 portions)

## 93. NORWEGIAN FISH SOUP

INGREDIENTS

2½-oz. packet of Norwegian       1 standard egg (well beaten)
  fish soup                      5-oz. carton soured cream

METHOD: Make the soup as directed on the packet; just before serving add the well-beaten egg and the soured cream, re-heat but do not boil. Serve hot.                    (4 portions)


## 94. HOT-SMOKED MACKEREL FILLETS

INGREDIENTS

1 packet Norwegian hot-          Brown bread and butter
  smoked mackerel fillets        Green salad with dressing
Wedge of lemon

METHOD: Open the packet 10 minutes before use, arrange on a plate with the salad, dressing and lemon. Eat with the bread and butter.                                  (1 portion)

# Picnic Ideas

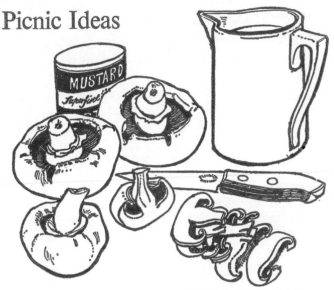

## 95. SOUR CREAM AND MUSHROOM SALAD

If you've never tried raw mushrooms in a salad you've missed a treat.

INGREDIENTS

3 oz. cucumber (peeled and diced)
3 hard-boiled eggs
4 oz. mushrooms
$\frac{1}{4}$ pint sour cream
$\frac{1}{2}$ level teaspoonful dry mustard

$\frac{1}{2}$ level teaspoonful grated horseradish
Salt and pepper to taste
4 tomatoes
Sprigs of parsley or watercress

METHOD: Into a basin put the cucumber, two diced hard-boiled eggs and the finely sliced mushrooms. In another basin blend the sour cream, mustard, horseradish and seasoning, then pour over the ingredients in the other basin. Turn the ingredients over gently with a spoon and stand in a cool place for at least 20 minutes. Arrange on a serving dish and garnish with the remaining sliced hard-boiled egg, tomatoes and parsley or watercress.                    (4 portions)

## 96. SALAD FOR ONE

Brown bread and butter goes very well with this salad.

INGREDIENTS

| | |
|---|---|
| 2 oz. diced Cheddar cheese | Pinch salt and pepper |
| 2 oz. diced cucumber | 2 lettuce leaves |
| ½ teaspoonful fresh lemon juice | 1 tomato |

METHOD: In a basin toss the cheese and cucumber together with the lemon juice and seasonings. Place the lettuce leaves on to a serving dish or plate, pile the salad into the centre, and garnish with the tomato. (1 portion)


## 97. ORIGINAL FRENCH DRESSING

Served with a crisp green salad, this dressing adds the finishing touch.

INGREDIENTS

| | |
|---|---|
| 1 part wine or best quality white vinegar | 3 parts finest salad oil Salt and pepper to taste |

METHOD: Mix all well together and serve sprinkled over salad. N.B. Lemon juice may be substituted for the vinegar if preferred or for diet reasons.


## 98. SAVOURY LOAF

To be eaten at home or out on a picnic, also good to eat when sitting round the fireside.

INGREDIENTS

| | |
|---|---|
| 1 small bloomer loaf | 1 oz. chopped toasted almonds |
| Approximately 2 oz. butter | |
| 4-oz. can salmon | Few lettuce leaves |
| 4 oz. cream cheese | |

METHOD: Cut the loaf into three slices lengthways, well butter, remembering to butter the centre slice on both sides. Mash the salmon and season to taste, then spread this on the bottom slice. Put the centre slice on top. Blend the cheese and almonds together and spread on to the centre slice, cover with a few lettuce leaves and press the top slice into place. Wrap closely in foil and store in a cool place until ready to serve. When serving cut in ample slices. (8–10 portions)

## 99. SLICED POTATO SALAD

A very nice potato salad using new potatoes.

Mix together in a basin some sliced cooked new potatoes with Danish mayonnaise, then add a little onion juice, salt and pepper, pinch of sugar, 1 teaspoonful vinegar and a few chopped chives. Mix all well together and serve.

## 100. CITRUS PUNCH

A very refreshing drink, especially chilled with a few ice cubes. A great favourite with children old and young!

INGREDIENTS

| | |
|---|---|
| 7 oz. granulated sugar | 2 oranges |
| $\frac{1}{2}$ pint cold water | 2 lemons |
| 2 grapefruit | Few cherries for decoration |

METHOD: Put the sugar and water into a saucepan, heat very slowly, stirring occasionally until the sugar has dissolved. Bring the syrup to the boil and then set aside to become quite cold.

In the meantime cut one or two slices of lemon and orange and reserve them for decoration. Squeeze the juice from all the fruit into a jug, add the cold syrup and stir well. Garnish with the orange and lemon slices and cherries, and a sprig of mint if desired. (6–8 glasses)

# Index